Cowboy Heart, Soul, and Humor

by

Doug Foshee

Leeann,
Hope you enjoy this!

Doug Foshee
07-31-07

Cowboy Heart, Soul, and Humor

Copyright 2006
by
Doug Foshee

ISBN 1-932196-81-1

WordWright.biz, Inc.
WordWright Business Park
46561 State Highway 118
Alpine, Texas 79830

Printed in the United States of America

To my wife, Clara.

Table of Contents

Introduction.. i
Good Sounds 1
The Birthday Question 3
A Dad's Advice..5
Huntin' Stories 7
Horse Traders..11
Red Top Cane 15
The Cross-Eyed Pool Player 19
Stressed 23
Look Twice 25
A Good Life 27
Close Encounters of the Cowboy Kind......................29
The Painting 33
Kindergarten Cowboy 35
New Boots..37
Old Blue Cat 39
Big Boy 41
Old Hats and Old Friends 43
Christmas Spurs and Milk Pen Calves.......................45
The Blacksmith and the Schoolteacher......................47
The Motto...51
The Real West..53
Some Confusion...55

Spurs and Bicycles..57
My Early Morning Wake-up Call.......................................61
Cowboy Garden 63
Time Stands Still...65
He Had a Way with Horses..67
An Old Cowboy's Wish...69
A Cowboy Morning 71
Starting the Day 73
Why are We Here?..75
The Drought 77
His Church 79
Are There Dogs and Horses in Heaven?............................81
God's Holy Place 83

Introduction

This book, *Cowboy Heart, Soul, and Humor* is a tribute to the cowboy way of life.

If you ask anybody that has ever cowboyed whether full time, part time, or even for a month, you'll soon realize that a true cowboy has a deep abiding love for that way of life, has just as deep a respect for God and the land, and has for sure seen some humor in it.

Some of these poems are from real events in my life, some are events in the lives of my friends, and some are just plain made up. I bet as you read them, you'll be reminded of someone you know, maybe yourself.

I hope this collection of poems bring a smile to your face or maybe, in some cases, a tear to your eye.

Sit back and enjoy!

Hope you have as much fun readin' 'em as I had writin' 'em.

Doug Foshee

Good Sounds

Sometimes I get to thinking about all the things that I
hold dear
Smelling fresh mowed hay, seeing a sunset, and the
everyday things I hear.

The sounds of my children laughing, a new calf when
it bawls,
The first nicker from a colt, my wife's footsteps
walking down the hall,
In church the organ music and the people when we
sing,
The old wood stove crackling, the first robin in the
spring.

The sound of company coming as they turn in at our
old gravel road,
The howling wind in winter when it's getting awful
cold,
The cows and calves at night time when the weaning's
just been done,
The sounds of young folks' voices when they're
having good clean fun.

Now all these things bring me great joy and that sure
ain't no spoof
But the grandest sound to my rancher's ears is rain on
my own tin roof.

The Birthday Question

The day that I turned fifty my wife decided to throw
Me a big bar-b-que so she invited most everybody we
did know.
She told them all to dress in black and to give me a real
hard time
To celebrate the passing of my youth and that I was
past my prime.

So the whole durn bunch they showed up to razz me
and to kid
By telling stories on me and to poke me in the ribs.
Some stories were funny, some were sad, and a few
best left untold
But we all had ourselves a real good time as the night
began to unfold.

We ate and laughed until near midnight when we
decided it should come to a stop.
Before all you good friends and neighbors leave I just
need to know, how'd I get over the hill without
ever reaching the top?

A Dad's Advice

As the cowboy's son was approaching manhood his
    daddy sat him down,
"Now, Son, you're growing up and you'll soon be
    spending more time in town
Looking the two-legged fillies over when you begin to
    try to find
The one to spend your life with so keep these things in
    mind.

It's sorta like picking a new horse from outa the whole
    durn bunch.
There's some certain qualities you have to decide on
    before you take the plunge.

Do I want one that's full of flash and shine but can't
make it when times get tough?
Or do I want one that's got heart and soul instead of all
that fluff?
What about a gal with faith in God and loves her Ma
and Pa,
And cares for others, has pride in her country and, Son,
now after all
You have to think about what you want to get out of
this here life
When you start considering what you really need while
looking for a wife.
One question there ain't no getting 'round before you
go out on the prowl,
Am I looking for a Mrs. Right or will I settle for a
Miss Right *now*!"

Huntin' Stories

On an elk hunt in New Mexico the fall of 2003
We was sittin' 'round the campfire when somebody
    began to speak,
"Boys, do you remember that elk hunt we had four
    years ago?
When we got up the second morning there was a foot
    of fresh new snow.
Well, old Ted and me we struck a hot track as soon as
    it was light.
I said I'll go to the left and you just make a circle
    'round to the right.
We'll push that old bull to one or the other (at least
    that was the plan).
I went uphill, got set up and waited at my
    predetermined stand.
After an hour and fifteen minutes with no bull or
    partner showing me their face
I just lit out toward where we had parked the Jeep
    before we began our chase.

I came to a spot where I could see old Ted had slipped
    and fell.
Tumbling down the slope end over end things had real
    quick gone to hell.
I found an arrow then farther on I found his hunting
    knife.
His cap had come off, one glove lay there. I feared for
    old Ted's life!

From the sign in the snow he had done about seven
    somersaults.
One boot lay up the hill, his other glove, too, I laughed,
    but it wasn't my fault.
Small trees he had tumbled over were barren of all
    their traces of snow.
It was an awful wreck that he was in but he never
    turned loose of his bow!"

The next guy around the campfire leaned back as if he
    was trying to think.
He smiled real big, picked up his coffee cup, and took
    himself a drink.
"Now, fellers, that's a good one but remember the
    turkey hunt the spring of '98?
It was cold and the creek was froze over as we drove in
    through the gate.
I went west and Mark went east of the roost we knew
    that was there.
We thought we could call some in if we split the
    gobblers from the rest of the pairs.

I didn't have to cross the creek and I got myself set up
　　quick as a flash.
Just as I sat down from the creek I heard this great big
　　loud splash.
Mark had broken through the ice clear up to his chin
　　and I began to laugh.
I told him, you silly fool get outa that creek. We ain't
　　got no time for you to take a bath!!"

One old boy was taking all this in when he just let out
　　a little chuckle.
"Some years back I was guiding a Yankee so fat he
　　needed a mirror just to see his own belt buckle.
He wanted a big mule deer buck to hang up on his
　　corporate office wall
But he was so outa shape he couldn't walk two
　　hundred yards without looking like he would fall.
He stayed as lost as a goose in a snowstorm as soon as
　　we got twenty feet from the truck
So we hoped that this last morning just might be the
　　one to change the fat boy's luck.

We parked along the road and he pulled out a little
　　weak flashlight.
He saw a real good buck in its beam and before I knew
　　it his arrow was fast in flight.
Then a porch light came on and a door swung open
　　with his arrow stuck smack dab in the middle.
That old fat boy out ran me to the truck. All of a
　　sudden he was fit as a fiddle!!"

As I listened to all these stories I knew as sure as I've got on my pants,

The conclusion is easy any way that you slice it; the first liar just don't stand a chance!!!

Horse Traders

We met up in South Texas some twenty years ago.
I don't recall his last name, but he answered to Elmo.
It was at the auction barn when some horses were just
    run in,
When he said, "I wouldn't allow them there nags to
    spend the night in my horse pens."

We talked them horses over and their qualities (which
    were mighty slim).
Then we cooked up a deal to look at his stock. To his
    place I'd follow him.
I knew from his look that he had some bargains but he
    had some surprises, too.
It was up to me to decide which was which in just a
    minute or two.

He had a little sorrel gelding that looked like he might
    do,
But the way he was priced you could have just as well
    bought yourself two!

We talked a while and when he thought he had the trap
well set
He run out a dapple mare and said, "Now, Son, she's
just a pet.
The little girl that had her lost interest in this mare
When she became a teenager and caused all the boys to
stare.
This mare is spirited and she'll move out, but her
disposition's kind.
I'd keep her for myself but my wife's already made up
my mind
To let her go to pay on some notes I've got down at the
bank,
Before they come and get me. You know, them
bankers get awful rank."

We got a halter on her, wiped her off with an old feed
sack,
Saddled her up and then I crawled up on her back.
She reared up, pawed at the moon and then broke in a
run.
I could tell right off that pets like her aren't a hell of a
lot of fun.

He said, "I can't believe it. That sweet little girl must
of lied."
When he told this tale to me he sounded like he was
about to cry.

We made a trade or two over the years and one thing I
found out to be true
When you deal with horse traders and I'll pass it on to
you.
You know that they are lying, about that there's no
doubt,
If their blasted mouth is moving and words are coming
out!!

Red Top Cane

In DeWitt County, Texas some years ago gone by
The winter grass was short. Summer had been awful dry.
To keep the cows from starving and the banker from
    going insane
We bought a couple semi loads of hay from red top
    cane.

We went to feeding red top cane hay every morning and
    at night.
Them old cows would come a runnin' when they'd see
    us pull in sight.

Now red top cane hay to those who haven't seen
Is pretty fair feed 'cept it can get a little mean.
To tell this tale to ladies so they won't set a howl
Let's just say that red top cane sure loosens up the
    bowels.

A heifer she was calving and was having a real tough go
So we kept a close eye on her for about an hour or so.
We put her up in the pens just in case we had to pull it
When we saw the old man come up the lane a' speeding
    like a bullet.

Now the old man he had a habit of hurry up and wait
But on this particular occasion he was running a little
     late.
"Hurry up boys!! Let's pull it quick. I'm gonna have to
     go!!
I promised the old lady I'd take her to town to see the
     picture show!!"

If the old man would've stayed away everything would
     have been just fine,
But he was the owner of this outfit and we knowed to
     walk the line!!

We got the pulling chains out and put the heifer in the
     chute.
The old man was barking orders and kicking dirt with
     the toe of his boot.

He finally bulled and bellered and said, "Just get
     yourself outa the way.
Right behind this heifer is where I'll be. We can't fool
     around all day!!"
In his haste he forgot the heifer had been on a diet of red
     top cane,
This oversight was a big mistake to him it would soon
     be plain.

When he strained to pull the calf out his mouth was
   open wide.
All of a sudden the after effects of red top cane hay then
   began to fly.
He didn't duck in time to miss what hit him square in
   the face.
With his mouth wide open he couldn't have been in a
   more distasteful place.

That calf arrived about that time. Newborn calves are
   always a pretty sight.
But the old man went to choking. We thought he'd gag
   all night.
His false teeth he had spit out which was a little risky.
At his pickup he was leaning, gargling with Jim Beam
   bourbon whiskey.
He rinsed his teeth and washed his mouth (used up
   nearly the whole blasted jug).
We laughed so hard we couldn't walk. We felt like we'd
   been drugged!

It's been over twenty years now since that heifer had
   that calf.
But if somebody mentions red top cane hay I'll just bust
   right out loud and laugh!!

The Cross-eyed Pool Player

One Saturday after payday we headed into town
To "turn our wolves loose" and to have ourselves a round.
Now the old boy that was with me was a pretty good shot
At the game of pool, however, I was sure not.

To the "Water Hole" we went with his cue stick in the truck
Him to hustle some poor sucker and with just a little luck
He'd soon have the money to pay off the note
On that brand new shop made saddle that he had just
    bought.

There at the pool tables was a cross-eyed old boy.
With his hat cocked back my pard's eyes filled with joy.
"That cross-eyed feller for my saddle he'll pay.
I'll set him up easy. You listen up to what I say."

I found me a stool to watch out this little story.
For that cross-eyed cowboy I was feeling just a little bit
    sorry.
They started out shooting for only a dollar a game.
After six games that old boy and my pard were tied up just
    the same.

"To make this game sporting," my buddy said, "let's up the
     ante to ten bucks."
That cross-eyed boy said, "Well, if you want to. It may
     even improve my luck."
To set him up for the kill my pard let him win three,
Then he said, "Double or nothing. How you think that'd
     be?"

Old cross-eyed he got lucky. (At least that's what we
     thought.)
As he won the last game my pard thought he ought
     To open up the stakes and go in for the kill.
Old cross-eyed's luck would soon be knocked out by his
     great shooting skill.

My pard told him, "Look I'm down sixty.
Let's shoot for a hundred, that is, if you don't think it's too
     risky.
To give you a chance I'll even let you have the break."
Old cross-eyed he just said, "Why, thank you. That's a
     chance I just think I'll take."

He screwed his hat down, then closed his left crossed eye.
Never such a shooter have I seen in my life.
Ten times he ran the table. We knew we'd been had.
It wasn't getting no better!! In fact it had got real bad!!
My pard tried backing out the door real quiet and slow
Without paying this cross-eyed pool shark. He just didn't
     know
Old cross-eyed now he was ready for just this kind of a
     trick,

When we heard the hammer of that old Colt 45 as cross-
    eyed thumbed it with a click.

We lost all our money, my pard's spare tire, and his brand
    new shop-made saddle.
I guess if we would have had a boat we'd even have lost
    the dad blasted paddle!

At pool you'll be sorry if a cross-eyed cowboy you'd rob.
If you're in need of money just go out and get yourself an
    extra *job*!

Stressed

We all feel stressed in our daily life.
It may be our job or husband or wife.

Our kids contribute to this stressful routine
Especially when they become a teen.

What to do or what to say.
I hope to get through this mess today.

But just remember when you get stressed
With our daily life and feel depressed
To put "stressed" in a mirror (it won't hurt.)
Stressed spelled backwards turns into *desserts!*

Look Twice

The first time I spied her
I eased up beside her.
My saddle was creaking.
I just started speaking.
When she sighed with a grin
Then it drooled down her chin.
I whirled and I scattered
For to me it shore mattered.
Cause there's something uncommon
'Bout a snuff dipping woman.

A Good Life

Once I had a horse named May.
She was honest and true and would work hard all day.
She did her best and was sound as a dollar
And was always willing when I called upon her.

A dog I once had who answered to Beau.
Would give all he had, always ready to go.

Then there's the woman, the love of my life.
Her name is Clara and she is my wife.
When I'm down she keeps my spirit up.
Well, I wouldn't trade her for a new speckled pup.

An old man once told me you've had a good life
If you've had a good horse, a good dog, and a good
        wife.

I'll go to my Maker as happy as could be
'Cause, boys, let me tell you I've had me all three.

Close Encounters of the Cowboy Kind

As I was coming back from town one night (I had been
    to the waterhole.),
I saw a funny looking light. It had a kinda green glow.
I eased my truck up to a stop. From the truck I eased as
    well.
Up to that funny green light I walked and to my knees
    I fell.

There in the pasture was a cow outfit right out there in
    plain sight.
But the whole danged outfit didn't stand but about two
    foot in total height.
I thought to myself two foot cowboys made my old
    eyes pop
When I see things like this my drinking days had best
    come to a stop.

Then all of a sudden one rode up and yelled out into
    the night,
"Get up you lazy bunch of hands. We're burning up
    moonlight."
From the bedrolls they jumped rubbing their eyes and I
    heard one of them say,
"Just once in my life I'd like to sleep the whole
    dadblasted day.
When you work for this brand it's dusk to dawn before
    you get any rest.
The day is short but the grub ain't bad but it dang
    shore ain't the best."

To the chuck wagon they staggered, to get their
    breakfast along with a steaming cup
Then grabbed their mounts and they all began to get
    them saddled up.
They rode out and I followed by the glow of that eerie
    looking green light.
As I went along I shore did see a peculiar looking
    sight.

They would rope rocks and logs and brush and stuff,
    turn them over and look around,
Jerk their ropes off, spur and head out right in the
    direction of town.

I watched all this 'till the sun started glowing off in the
      eastern sky.
When back to camp they rode. Their spirits shore
      weren't very high.

I'd been real quiet and had not been seen when I
      stepped on a stick and it cracked.
Those green cowboys had me roped and tied. They
      shore didn't cut me no slack.

The boss rode up and asked me was spying what I did
      for my trade.
I told him cowboying was what I did for the wages that
      I made.

They let me loose and told me to get, they had things
      they had to get done.
I could see they weren't mean so we talked a while and
      had us a lot of fun.
"Before I get gone there's a question I gotta ask that's
      got my old head a swimming'
What are you looking under all that stuff for?" They
      said with a wink,
"Fool, we're looking for *little green women!*"

The Painting

I once saw a painting where a man roped a bear.
An experience like that I thought I might want to share.
Of bears there were none and none nowhere near.
So I says to myself, "I'll just rope me a deer."

I saddled up early and pulled it up real tight.
I had no idea I'd end up in such a fight.

To Dead Indian Mountain pasture went my pony and
    me
With my rope tied hard hoping a deer we might see.
We rode in that pasture for an hour or such
When I saw a big deer with his head behind some
    brush.

I spurred and we took off. Boys, this will be fun!
I swung and I threw as he started to run.
As the loop went around the horns I pitched in my
    slack.
He hit the end running and then he looked back.
The fire in his eyes made my blood run cold
For being so foolish, stupid, and bold.

The next things that happened are still kinda hazy.
But when I woke up I felt somewhat crazy.
My old pony was gone. The deer was nowhere in sight.
I then took the time to look over my plight.

My pants were in tatters. My shirt was plumb gone.
I had scratches and hoof prints all over and I ached to
the bone.

Back to the headquarters was a long eleven miles
And going afoot, I was wearing no smiles.
I learned me a lesson they don't teach you in school.
Folks who believe all them paintings are a bunch of
dern fools!!

Kindergarten Cowboy

In the house the little boy walked. To his Dad he said,
"I'll have no more schooling. I'm going to bed."

This set the man back. Of his son he wanted to know
Why after just one week of Kindergarten to no more
schooling he'd go.
The man told his son to come over and sit,
"Before you bail out, let's talk us a bit."

The son politely told him, "Dad, we don't have to
fight.
I can already count some. My name I can write.
That school house is stuffy and boring as can be.
A cowboy like you is my goal, don't you see?
You can teach me 'bout horses and cattle and such.
The life I'd be living couldn't be better luck."

The Dad he just sat there and said with a grin,
"Son, my footsteps you'll follow, but school's where
you'll begin."

New Boots

The bottoms of his boots were thin. The tops were shot
    as well.
He could step on a dime and he knew right away if it
    was laying heads or tails.
To the boot shop he went to get himself a new pair.
The boot maker said, "Come on in! Pull up a chair!"
We'll measure you out, you pick out a hide.
Your foot I'll fit whether narrow or wide.
I'll guarantee comfort," he said in a holler,
"If they don't suit, I'll return every dollar!!"

Well, time went by, the new boots were done.
They arrived in the mail about the set of the sun.

The old rancher wore them near 'bout a week.
When he went to town he heard the boot maker speak,
"How's them new boots? Bet they fit like a glove!
That leather's as soft as your own mother's love!!"

The old man, he spoke and looked him in the eye,
"Well, Pard, you asked me and I shore won't lie.
The boots hurt my feet. My blisters are sore.
They're the most uncomfortable pair of boots I ever
    have wore!!"

The boot maker said to the man with a sigh,
"Turn 'em back in!! That pair you won't buy!!"

The old rancher said, "The boots will stay mine.
They hurt like the devil, but they'll do me just fine.
Now listen up, sir, and I'll try to explain.
From the time I wake up my whole day's one big
      strain.

Cow prices are low. Feed bills are high.
My old horse is lame. The creek's durn near dry.
My dog's got the mange. My wife's a big nag.
My mother-in-law moved in (blasted old hag).
My note at the bank is way past due.
My son's in jail and my daughter's late too!!

Right now the only pleasure I get out of life
Is knowing these boots will come off at night!!!"

Old Blue Cat

This here is a story 'bout an old cat I once knew.
He was cross-eyed and ornery and his color was blue.
He lived way out back behind the horse barn
'Cause we'd see that old scoundrel just about every
    morn.

He kept his distance from all us except old Slick
Who didn't like cats so he'd greet him with a kick.
The blue cat was persistent about that there's no
    mistake
But friends with Slick it was impossible to make.

Now Slick cared 'bout horses, kids, cattle, and dogs.
He had no use at all for cats, snakes, or hogs.
The old cat kept trying to make Slick his friend
But Slick's aloofness brought about a bitter end.

One evening at sundown near the old windmill pump
Hid that old blue cat, just waiting to jump.
Slick was bringing in some dry cows to the North
    shipping pens
When that cat lit behind Slick's saddle and dug his
    claws in.

39

That young colt came unhinged and jumped for the
    road
But Slick stuck with him. He didn't want to unload
'Cause that old ranch road was lined up with plenty
    prickly pear
And that old cat was a' sittin' that colt like he was in a
    soft rocking chair.

Now Slick might have bucked him out if that old cat
    hadn't squalled.
Made the hair stand up on my head and I'm nearly
    bald.
With all this commotion Slick got throwed on his head.
When we got up to him we thought he was dead.
His eyes finally opened. From his mouth teeth were
    spat.
He said, "Boys, listen up now, I better make friends
    with that cat!"

Big Boy

In Cuero, Texas during the Great Gobbler Roundup
A parade was to be held. I got there about sunup.
I rode my horse Big Boy, an old sorrel nag
Who to my knowledge never carried a flag.
He was ranch raised and solid, so I said I would
Carry the flag. I figured he'd do what he should.

We lined up on a side road. (Horses always went last.)
So bands marching by wouldn't step in the groceries
    they'd passed.
Horse biscuits are natural and just part of life,
But on band uniforms and shoes, it may cause you
    some strife.

With the flag at attention I was soon to discover
Of a big bass drum, that old horse was no lover.
The drummer went to banging as he got even with us
And old Big Boy came unglued and started a fuss.

He spun to the right. The flag covered his face.
That asphalt sure looked hard. I thought I'd ended my
     race.
I tried to whoa him. I spurred hard his right shoulder.
That old fool stopped dead in his tracks. I was getting
     no bolder.

We finally marched on and got our part done.
That old pony was buggered throughout the whole run.
I made God a promise I've kept 'till this day.
Get me through this thing in one piece, Lord, and I'll
     ride in no more parades.

Old Hats and Old Friends

My wife's a fine lady. There's no doubt about that.
But she has no understanding 'bout my old cowboy
    hat.

Hats are a lot like people though
We don't like to think it so.
When it's new it don't feel quite right
Like a little child when they're crying all night.

Then after you've had it a while it feels like it's earned
    its place
Like a young man that's just starting his run in life's
    race.
Then after the hat's weathered and worn and survived
    many storms
Its like a loved one whose touch is comfortable and
    warm.

Now there's no use to desert a hat 'cause it shows a
    little age
No sooner than you'd desert a friend who's about to
    turn his life's last page.

So, Pard, remember what I'm saying because these
  words are true,
"Old hats and old friends will be there 'cause they're
  loyal through and through."

Christmas Spurs and Milk Pen Calves

When I was just a button, for Christmas I got
Some spurs and some leggings. Boy, I was hot!!
I thought bull riding would be kinda neat
But I'd start on milk pen calves to accomplish my feat.

The folks went to town and didn't make us go
So we had all morning for our own little rodeo.
My cousin and I'd run a calf into the chute
Wrap a rope around his girth and let out a whoop!!

We'd ride each calf some until we got throwed
When all of a sudden we saw dust coming up the road.

About then my cousin got pitched right into the barn.
I laughed real loud, wasn't worried about harm.
He hit his head hard. He was out like a wedge.
I drug him outta the pen where right near the edge
Was a big old cottonwood with a rope swing hanging
      there.
I was afraid he was dead so I let up a prayer.

He started to come to and quick we made up a tale
'Cause for riding those calves we knew we'd catch
    hell.
We said from the tree he had taken a fall.
The story we told was believed by one and all.

Next morning real early my uncle and Dad
Said, "Get out here you boys!!" We knew they were
    mad!
"Spur marks in these calves hair just didn't grow.
You boys told a windy of this we now know!"

Our britches got tanned good for telling a lie.
They told us, "Be honest. Look a man in the eye!"
It's been years since my cousin and I made our big
    mistake.
We learned our lesson. Honesty is always the best road
    to take!

The Blacksmith and the Schoolteacher

The blacksmith and the schoolteacher looked like they
    was head over heels in love.
As they held hands any fool could tell they were star
    struck from up above.
He was tall and slim and strong and spoke with a kinda
    bashful drawl.
She was short and pretty and looked just like a little
    China doll.

To think of that team hitched to the wagon together
    sure seemed like a mismatched pair
But they loved each other so much that they didn't
    even give a care.
They planned on the wedding to take place the last
    week into June.
Then they'd take off for a few days to have their
    honeymoon.

When they got back they talked like they'd each found
   the perfect spouse.
She went right to work making their home in what was
   once the blacksmith's house.
She scrubbed and cleaned out the last remains of what
   used to be his bachelorhood.
The old place shined like new money. It never looked
   so good.

As summer ended and school began the schoolteacher
   told folks around,
"He's the best husband in the world. He's good and
   true and you know what I found?
He gets up early every morning cooks and washes his
   plate and skillet up
Then wakes me with a gentle kiss and brings me coffee
   in a cup."

Well, to those of us who knew that feller in his
   younger days were set back with surprise.
"That don't sound like the ways old Bill had back then,
   but that pretty young gal wouldn't lie!"

Things rocked along for a couple of months when the
   teacher came in one day.
She was fit to be tied, throwing a hissy fit and she
   began to say,
"I got to feeling guilty about Bill cleaning up after
   breakfast while I slept.
I planned to take care of it for him so into the kitchen I
   crept,
Just in time to see him take from the floor his skillet
   and his plate
After his old cow dog Duke had licked them clean as
   from both of them he ate.

I came uncorked and yelled and screamed about filth
   and germs and such."
Old Bill, he just stood there calmly and then he just
   kinda backed up.
"Now, Marilyn," he said, "there ain't no use for you to
   yell and fuss and fret.
I've knowed old Duke longer than I've knowed you
   and his germs ain't killed me yet."

The Motto

When I was just a young kid all full of buck and bawl
I hired out to be a cowboy 'cause I shore thought I
    knew it all.
In my mind I could outdo all the older men and I was
    not shy to tell
To everyone that would listen that I was tough as nails.

I did okay for a few months and worked mostly my big
    mouth.
Then I ran into some real tough broncs and everything
    went south!
I crawled into my "pity sack" full of gloom and great
    despair.
There just was not one thing in this old life that treated
    me halfway fair.

Then I met up with an old puncher that always had a
    smile.
The boys would gouge and tease him but he would go
    the extra mile.

One day they wrapped up a box of horse manure with
      paper and a bow
And told him they got him a present to open at home
      and not to show
Anyone else what was in it because it was a surprise
To be seen only by him and no one else's eyes.

The next day they asked him, "How was your gift that
      did not smell quiet like a bouquet of posies?"
He smiled and said, "Oh, I didn't like it much, but it
      was good for my wife's roses!

When times get rough and you are dealt some pretty
      rotten cards
You can moan and whine and fuss and cuss how life is
      awful hard.
But this I choose as my motto, boys, and this shore
      ain't no bull,
I don't see the glass as half empty, I see the thing as
      being halfway *full*!"

The Real West

The western movies and TV show life as one big party
But to live back then the folks and stock shore had to
be awful hardy.

Roy Rogers and Gene Autry never sweated or got
dirty.
Their shiny boots and saddles, fancy shirts, and guitars,
(and guns that never needed reloading) made
cowboy life seem real pretty.
Their saddlebags held everything they needed out on
the lonely plains,
Dutch ovens, coffee pots, food galore, and tarps if it
came a rain.
Somehow they managed to fit in other things along
with their guitars
So they had a full orchestra in the background as they
sang at night to the shining stars.

White hats always meant good guys, the bad ones they
    wore black.
The hero won the battles, tipped his hat and never
    looked back.
The fair maiden that he rescued sighed smiling as he
    up and rode away
'Cause she knew she was his one true love and he'd be
    back some day.

Now that's the way they show it upon the silver screen
When in reality life in the real west had some times
    that were pretty lean.
Most folks had no fancy ranch house sitting high upon
    a hill
With lots of cowboys in the bunkhouse to work and do
    their will.
The work was done by themselves or it just did not get
    done.
Each day they were out from daylight to well past the
    setting of the sun.

The men (and some women) took care of the livestock
    and "outside chores" each day.
The women folks cooked, took care of the kids, made
    the clothes (with no neighbors to visit) and taught
    the kids to pray.

I've heard it said before from some very reliable
    sources,
"That life in the real west was hard on men and dogs,
    but it was hell on women and horses."

Some Confusion

Some folks believe they have the right to just "tell it
   like it is"
Whenever and wherever to me it is a quiz.
Anything coming from their mouth to them it is OK.
Why should they ever worry about what THEY might
   have to say?

Things like, "My, but ain't she getting fat!"
And, "Dear Lord! I wouldn't be caught dead wearing
   such a hat!"
And shore 'nuff zingers they'll blab out just every now
   and then
Like, "My God, she looks like the Goodyear blimp
   when she used to be so thin!!"
And, "She sings in church just like a bird. Yeah, a big
   old cacklin' hen!"

And, "If I hear him tell that same old story just one
   more time again
One or both of us will have to go right straight to the
   looney bin!!"
And, "Her house looks like a big old storm has just
   passed through right there!"

And, "With kids like theirs I shore am proud they quit
  when they had the pair!"

It leads to some confusion I'll tell you right up front,
Why do we refer to a "sharp-tongued woman" as her
  "just being blunt"?!

Spurs and Bicycles

Now spurs is a great invention for cueing horses and
   such
But when it comes to riding bicycles they don't bring
   about much luck.
The story I'm fixin' to tell you was told to me as true,
So if it was a windy, then a windy I'll be telling you.

He'd just come in 'bout ten o'clock from making his
   morning round
When he saw the dust a comin', his wife had been to
   town.
It was his little girl's birthday and he had been saving
   his money
For her a brand new bicycle, a red one, and it shore
   was a honey.

His wife stopped in front of the house with this red
   bicycle in the back.
He unhitched the ropes, put it out, and wiped the dust
   off with an old feed sack.
Now all this time the little girl had been peeking out
   the door.

She came running out, "Is it for me?" She couldn't
　　stand it any more.

She looked it over and got aboard while her daddy held
　　it steady.
Then she got scared and told him she just didn't think
　　she was ready.
He told her, "Now look here you won't get hurt, you
　　don't need be afraid.
I'll ride it first. See it's easy." (Boy what a mistake he
　　made.)

It had been many years since he had ridden anything
　　but a horse
So the spurs on his boots were always there just as a
　　matter of course.
The road sloped down to the creek so that's the way
　　he'd go.
When he got up a head of steam out of habit he
　　hollered, "Whoa!!"

The bicycle kept a going and picked up a lot of speed.
He had to stop or go in the creek, of a bath he had no
　　need.
Well, things got to happening faster and he ended up in
　　the dirt.
The bicycle was okay but old Dad's pride was sorta
　　hurt.

Mom and the little girl run up to help him from this
  awful wreck.
When he jumped up and told them, "I'll get this thing
  in check.
Now for twenty years of my life horses I have
  wrangled.
I'm glad they don't have spokes for my spurs to get
  entangled!"

That little girl is married now and moved off on her
  own.
She's thought about Dad's bicycle lesson now that
  she's up and grown.
It's time to teach her daughter to ride the bike that once
  was hers.
But before she does she'll be sure to take off that
  blasted pair of spurs!

My Early Morning Wake-up Call

We saddled up just before sunrise to make ourselves a
　　drive.
That special time of morning when everything seems
　　to come alive.
The air felt cool and fresh as we rode out to start our
　　day.
I guess I was still kinda half asleep as we went along
　　our way.

The horse that I was riding this morn was still a good
　　deal green.
Now he weren't no outlaw or anyway near what you
　　might call rank or mean.
He was just a little cold backed and had to give about a
　　dozen jumps
When you first crawled up on him, I guess, just to
　　straighten out his hump.

We got past his morning rituals and was going along
   just right
When I heard a locust key up like they do sometimes at
   night.
The sound I thought was a locust brought about a big
   surprise.
'Cause coiled right under my horse buzzed a rattler
   that was not lacking at all for size!
Now this old pony he went to bucking and trying to
   leave this place.
I don't blame him at all for his efforts, but I shore
   didn't want to loose this race.

The other boys were laughing hard as they watched
   this little rodeo.
I guess I stayed on pretty good, at least I seemed to
   think so.
That blasted horse pitched so hard that I began to
   cough.
I lost both my stirrups but I never did go quiet all the
   way off.

This little wake-up call got my attention as I looked
   down at the ground.
When you think it's a locust singing it might be a
   "Texas buzz lizard" that's making *his* awful
   sound!

Cowboy Garden

When my wife and me got married in the year of '85
She wanted me to plow and plant a garden, which to
    me came as a big surprise.
Why, don't that gal know I'm a cowboy and a plow
    don't fit my hands?
I thought that sure ain't gonna happen to me, but now I
    wear her brand!

After grumbling and griping a plow I borrowed from a
    man I knew with a farm.
If my cowboy buddies don't know about this I guess it
    won't do me no permanent harm.
The ground got busted up and laid out in neat and tidy
    rows.
The seeds were planted and about half of them was eat
    up by a bunch of blasted crows.

After my long day of plowing and planting I figured
    my "farmin" work was done.
Then I was taught about watering and hoeing and bugs
    and all other sorta fun.
I thought you was through after you plowed and
    planted them little bitty seeds.
I just never knew one patch of ground could grow so
    many dadgum weeds!!

The beans, corn, peppers, squash, and tomatoes were
    finally ready for eatin'
And all this good food come out of our very own little
    special Garden of Weedin'!!

Time Stands Still

The first time I saw that young lady she was facing
    away from me.
Atop her long blonde hair sat a Stetson hat. She wore
    some tight fittin' jeans.
My heart was stole away from me to that I must
    confess.
I heard wedding bells ringing with me standing there
    and her in a long white dress.

Even though I had not yet spoke to her I knew she'd be
    my one true love.
I thought she must be an angel sent down to me from
    the heavens so far up above.
I stood there shaking in my boots with my heart agoing
    flip-flop.
Then she turned and I saw that her beauty wouldn't
    make time stand still but her looks could shore
    stop a clock!

He Had a Way With Horses

The first time that I met him he'd just turned eight-one.
The creases in his face and his weathered hands
    showed he had seen the rise and set of many a sun.
I had heard stories about him that when in his younger
    day
He had a reputation with horses to have a special way.

Now as I sat down with him I saw a look in his eyes
When I mentioned horses about them he'd not be shy.
He told me stories of when in his youth he topped out
    the rough ones
On ranches in the area from daylight to the set of the
    evening sun.

Some of the cowboys in that day had a harsh and brutal
    hand
But this old boy used his skill and patience on the
    horses that wore his brand.
"The trick", he said, "is to teach 'em what to do or not
    to do
But you gotta be as smart as the horse to get the lesson
    through.
Never break their spirit, boy, 'cause a horse shore has a
    soul.

If his spirit's broke, he's as worthless as a bucket with
a hole."
As we walked out back toward the old pens and barn
His memories stirred of days he'd spent there
beginning in early morn.
"It won't be long now before I pass this world and
leave this here old life
Of aches and pains and doctor bills, high taxes and
other strife.

I hope when I meet Him there as I stand before the
Pearly Gates
He points me toward a horse barn, and says, 'Son,
come on in, let's not wait.
I know your ways, I've seen your life that now has run
its courses.
You're what I need up here in heaven 'cause you've
got a way with horses.'"

An Old Cowboy's Wish

My steps are a little slower.
My shoulders droop a little lower.
My eyes have seen things
That make my heart sing.
But the things that I remember the best
Are the days I spent out in the West.

I've seen the Marfa lights.
I've seen young bulls fight.
I've seen the sun set slowly.
I've heard a calf bawl lowly.
I've felt a good horse between my knees.
I've been cooled by a mountain breeze.
I've felt a rope as it jerked up tight.
I've eaten camp grub well before daylight.

When I pass this life and meet my Boss
I pray He gives me a good stout horse.
Looks me over and in His strong voice
Says, "Son, today, I've made My choice.
Get on your horse and ride over My land
Because to Me you're one of My top hands.
Now I know that Texas is where you'd rather be
But, Pard, you're in heaven, now you're riding for *me.*"

A Cowboy Morning

When old Coosie* banged on the bell about 4:30 today
I said to myself, "My gosh, I just now hit the hay!!"
To pull the covers up and stay in my bedroll would
    sure be grand
But yesterday the foreman had already laid out a plan.

"We'll get up, grub up, and meet at the horse pens at
    five.
Saddle up and ride out and work ourselves a drive.
You boys better eat up at breakfast 'cause we won't be
    back 'till dark.
It's a long ride over rough country so pick out a horse
    with heart.

This drive, it ain't for slackers and I won't be looking
    back.
You signed on to work as cowboys and today might
    split the pack.
Rexall Rangers and Barbershop Buckaroos always fail
    and fade away
But the top hands stick it out and do the job all day."

Now cow camp grub for breakfast ain't fancy but it's
     usually hot.
Fried steak, eggs, and taters, cathead biscuits and
     coffee by the pot.
I stuffed in all I could eat and ambled to the pens.
It wasn't even breaking light as the foreman reined his
     big bay in.

He bellered as he rode up, "Let's go, boys! We're
     burning light!"
I thought but did *not* say, "You crazy fool, it's still the
     middle of the night!!"

We were about three miles from headquarters when in
     the east began a glow.
That special time of morning when those who work the
     land always know
This life's a whole lot better than working from nine to
     five in any town.
To see what we see daily would wipe away *any* frown.

Then I saw the mist up high rising and I felt my old
     heart say,
"God's breathing life into His mountains. Thanks,
     God, for another day!"

*Coosie is the nickname for a camp cook. The word comes
from the Spanish word for cook—cosinero.*

Starting the Day

I awoke to the smell of bacon frying on this, another
day
And I listened to the others stirring and what they had
to say.

Old Bill, he just lay there moaning as he covered his
head up.
Sam he jumped right up smiling and said, "Hey,
Cookie, how 'bout a cup??!!
Your coffee it ain't for the weak of soul but I guess
I've tasted worse.
If a man drank more than a cup or two he just might
need a hearse,
But your grub ain't too bad to sit down to if you ain't
to awful weak-hearted
It'll open your eyes and scald your throat and help
your old body get jump-started!!"

Now Pete is getting up in years and has been in some
pretty bad wrecks
So his bones they creak and pop as he moves about
trying to get hisself in check.
Glenn just keeps right on sleeping with his loud roof
rattling snoring.
A bunk house might not be a 5-star hotel but it durn
sure ain't ever boring.

One young cowboy came in late last night from his
　　howling at the moon.
"Just once," he moaned, "I wished I had a job that
　　would let me sleep 'till noon!!"

Then softly we heard an old cowpoke as he bent down
　　on his knees,
"Lord, thanks for the good night's rest, my health, and,
　　Sir, now if you would please,
Give us all the strength that we will need to make it
　　through the day,
And be a friend to all your critters. For this I humbly
　　pray."

I figured out something that I don't think will be a big
　　mistake.
You can tell the sort that a feller is when he just first
　　comes awake.

Why are We here?

It had been a long hard day and the branding and
     working the calves was finally done.
After supper we sat on the porch when all of a sudden
     a question was asked by my son.
"Dad," he asked, "Why do you reckon that we've been
     put here to spend our time on this old earth?
I mean, what's it all about and what are we supposed
     to do with the time we've got before we die and
     after our birth?"

It took me by surprise a question like that from a kid
     just twelve years old.
So I sure thought about what to say before the words
     from my mouth began to flow.
"Now, son, this question I've pondered over and over
     myself in my own mind
And the way that I see it is how I'll try to settle the
     answer you're trying to find.

I figure each one of us here has a place in God's own
     master plan
Or why else would He have gone to all the trouble to
     create this thing that He calls "man".
He must of thought pretty high of us 'cause He allows
     us to make our own choices.
I reckon if He had wanted to He could have just made
     us like string puppets and added in some voices.

75

But He gives us the chance each day to do what's right
or what's wrong.
We can follow His laws, be honest and fair, or be part
of the crowd and just tag along.
Son, even if we try to do our very best as we pass
along this way.
That ain't quite good enough to get our hides past them
old Pearly Gates.
So He sent His son to die for our sins on that cruel old
rugged cross.
But we've got to accept that gift of His or, son, for
eternity we'll sure 'nuff be lost.

I guess the best way to answer the question of why we
were put here on this place
Is that we're here to make God happy and please Him
and that puts a big smile upon His face.
We do that by accepting His love and trying to make a
hand for Him each and every day,
By keeping His commandments, loving our neighbor,
and asking for His guidance whenever we pray.

Then when this life is over and they lay our body down
underneath this old earthly sod
We'll be happy in Heaven 'cause we know that forever
we'll be held in the loving arms of our God."

The Drought

Several years ago the circuit preacher rode into our
    little town.
Instead of a warm welcome he was just met with a
    bunch of frowns.
"Why are you so glum and sad on this God's glorious
    day?"
"Well, Preacher, can't you see the rain's just gone
    away?
We ain't had a drop at all since way back last
    November
And here it is just three days shy of the first week in
    September.
The grass is short, the creeks dried up, the old well
    won't hardly even pump.
Feed is high, cow prices low, Preacher, we're in an
    awful slump!!"
The preacher smiled and bowed his head and then
    began to pray,
"Lord, thank You for the gifts You give to us each and
    every day.
We're quick to moan and groan about what we think
    that we are missing
Without remembering what You always do for us with
    all Your wonderful blessings.

You've told us in Your Holy Word how You will
    always be sufficient
But we soon forget and think that somehow You have
    become deficient.
We thank You now for the rains You'll be sending to
    us not later but quicker.
We trust Your love so much that in the middle of a
    drought we'll all start carrying our slickers!"

His Church

His Church is more than just a building where
    people come and sit
To gossip with the other folks and show how
    their new clothes fit.

His church is God's holy place where believers
    sing and pray
And ask Him for His guidance as we go about
    our way.

It's like believers that have joined together with
    a bond that we all share,
Our fellowship and heartaches that we all
    sometimes bear.

It's where we learn about His love that is so
    great and true.
Of His son's death and resurrection. His
    ultimate gift to me and you.

So when we come together to share His holy
    word
We are His church and we are truly in the
    presence of the Lord.

Are there Dogs and Horses in Heaven?

As I sat on my porch last night thinking about all the
    things that go on in this life,
The good and the bad, the happy and sad, and our joys
    and struggles and strife.
A thought just kept on circling 'round the hollows of
    my old feeble head.
Will our good dogs and horses meet us up there in
    heaven as we walk through the Gates when we're
    dead?

The Bible I took off the shelf to seek the answer in
    God's own Holy Book.
I read and I read but nothing could I find no matter
    how hard I did look.
I went to bed with more questions than answers and
    tried to get me some sleep.
After tossing and turning and flipping and flopping
    with no rest that was near halfway deep
I sat up in bed with my eyes wide open and I heard His
    voice speak and He said,
"Now, Son, this question of good dogs and horses
    that's going around in your head

I'll answer for you if you'll just listen to these words of
    mine from up above.
The secret to a living thing having a soul is that if the
    critter is loved.

I gave mankind a soul on the day I created you 'cause I
    loved you from deep in My heart
But you broke My laws by your sins and from the
    Garden you had to depart.

So I sent down my Son to give His life for you to die
    on that old rugged cross.
My love was so strong that I didn't think about it no
    matter how great was the cost.

Now all critters don't have souls but those that have
    someone to love them and that they love too
Are granted a soul because that great love is just the
    same way that I love you.
If they pass on before you they'll be in a sleep until
    your life's clock has run its courses.
Then waiting at the Gates will be the ones you loved;
    Me, good dogs, and good horses."

God's Holy Place

As I gaze out over the mountains, I feel I'm in
    God's Holy Place.
The sights, the sounds, the cool fresh breeze
    brings a smile to my old weathered face.

I ask Him to be with me each day as I try to
    preserve His great land.
To guide my thoughts and deeds as I strive to be
    one of His hands.

I know, Lord, I'm not very worthy of favors to
    be granted you see
But when You look in Your great tally book,
    please leave a place open for me.

About the Author
Doug Foshee

Doug spent eleven years as a speech therapist and twenty-one years as a principal in Texas public schools. In 1993, he attended his first Cowboy Poetry Gathering in Alpine, Texas, and that set him off writing his own cowboy poetry. During his time off from teaching, he cowboyed on ranches in South Texas.

He says of himself, "I was born at a very young age in Harris County, Texas. I spent the first twenty years of my life there and never once felt dry, so each time I moved, I ended up further West from the coast."

Doug and his wife Clara have lived in Alpine, Texas since 1992.

This book, *Cowboy Heart, Soul, and Humor* depicts Doug's respect and love for the cowboy way of life.

To order additional copies of
Cowboy Heart, Soul, and Humor

Name _____

Address _____

_____

_____

$12.95 x _____ copies = _____

Sales Tax   _____
(Texas residents add 8.25% sales tax)

Please add $3.50 postage and handling   _____

Total amount due: _____

Please send check or money order for books to:

WordWright.biz, Inc.
WordWright Business Park
46561 State Highway 118
Alpine, Texas 79830

For a complete catalog of books,
visit our site at
http://www.WordWright.biz

Printed in the United States
48189LVS00001B/196-237

9 781932 196818